95

INTERRACIAL DATING AND MARRIAGE

INTERRACIAL DATING AND MARRIAGE

ELAINE LANDAU

JULIAN MESSNER

JULIAN MESSNER and colophon are trademarks of Simon
& Schuster.
Project Editor: Yvonne Lucas
Design: Anne Ricigliano
Photos: J. Gerard Smith

Manufactured in the United States of America.

Lib. ed. 10 9 8 7 6 5 4 3 2 1
Paper ed. 10 9 8 7 6 5 4 3 2 1

Library of Congress Cataloging-in-Publication Data

Landau, Elaine.
    Interracial dating / by Elaine Landau.
        p. cm.
    Includes bibliographical references and index.
    Summary: Surveys the history of interracial dating and marriage
and presents the experiences of young people and adults involved in
such relationships.
    1. Interracial dating—United States—Public opinion—Juvenile
literature.   2. Public opinion—United States—Juvenile literature.
3. Teenagers—United States—Attitudes—Juvenile literature.
[1. Interracial dating—Personal narratives.   2. Interracial marriage—
Personal narratives.]   I. Title.
HQ801.8.L36   1993
306.73—dc20   92-44814
                                                                   CIP
                                                                   AC

ISBN 0-671-75258-8 (LSB)
ISBN 0-671-75261-8 (pbk.)

Contents

Introduction

Emmett Till was a fourteen-year-old African American from Chicago, Illinois. In 1955, he was visiting relatives in Mississippi when he asked a young white woman for a date. Outraged by his request, the woman refused and angrily relayed what had happened to her husband and his half brother. That night the two men barged into the house where Till was staying and ordered him from his bed at gunpoint. After pistol-whipping the boy, they shot him and threw his body into the Tallahatchie River. Although both men later confessed to the cold-blooded murder, an all-white, male jury refused to convict them.

Emmett Till's case was not an isolated incident. Unfortunately, African-American and white interpersonal relations have a long history characterized by violence and abuse. The groundwork for racism was laid in the early days of our nation. Beginning in the 1660s, and continuing through the early portion of the eighteenth century, legislatures devised codes and laws to solidify the distinction between slaves and free individuals, and to discourage mixed marriages. In designing these laws, they tried to define precisely who was not white. An individual was generally considered a "Negro" if he or she were one-eighth African or had a single great-grandparent believed to be of African descent.

In 1741, for example, North Carolina passed the following statute: "For prevention of that abominable mixture and spurious issue, which hereafter may increase in this government, by white men and women intermarrying with Indians [during the colonial period, some Native Americans were enslaved, and a number of these individuals had some African ancestry], Negroes, Mustees [the offspring of a white person and a person who is one-quarter African], or Mulattoes, be it enacted . . . that if any white man or woman being free shall intermarry . . . he shall, by judgment of the county court forfeit and pay the sum of fifty pounds." The designated fine was sufficiently large to force free men or women to sell themselves into bondage (as indentured servants) in order to pay it.

Laws against intermarriage varied from state to state. In some areas, a mixed marriage was a criminal offense punishable by up to ten years in prison in addition to a hefty fine. In several states, the clerk who issued the marriage license and the clergyman who performed the ceremony were jailed as well.

Both state and federal courts consistently upheld statutes prohibiting interracial unions. Even white men wishing to adopt children born to them by African-American women were denied the right to do so. Judges argued that such adoptions would sanction interracial unions.

Although many whites were opposed to interracial romance, they especially feared mixed marriages. While having sexual relations with whites afforded African Americans no genuine status, marriage was a legal contract between equals. Granting legal status to Africans on any level posed a serious threat to slavery and the Southern economy.

Following the American Revolution, most Northern states abolished slavery. But much of the North still placed legal limits on African-American freedoms, including the right to marry whites. As the Union grew, Plains and Western states also adopted laws against interracial marriages. Eventually, thirty out of forty-eight states banned mixed marriages. Many retained these statutes until the late 1940s.

Even where interracial marriage wasn't outlawed, mixed couples might face serious consequences within their communities. In the 1850s, a visitor from England to Buffalo, New York, described the plight of an interracial couple he met as follows. "The wife [a white woman] was despised by the wives of white citizens, and both [the husband and wife] were shunned. White etiquette would not let him attend her at the theater box; they never ventured out together. If they did go out, it was usually after dark. On one occasion, the man was mobbed and nearly lost his life."

In the middle of the nineteenth century, when Joseph Woodman, an African-American Arkansan and his white fiancée went north to marry, he hadn't realized that his life was at risk. But word of the couple's intentions had reached the sheriff's office, and before the two of them had gotten very far, they were arrested by the lawman's posse. The woman was returned to her parents' home, but Woodman supposedly was to spend the night in jail. Instead, the young man was murdered later that evening. The next morning his body was found hanging from a tree.

Violence stemming from interracial liaisons was not confined to the South. In 1867, a young African-American Westerner named William Dixon was arrested when he tried to kiss a white girl. After being kicked, tortured, and tarred and feathered, he was left in the desert to die.

Despite the consequences, however, mixed marriages persisted in America. An 1880 census indicates that there were 209 interracial married couples in New Orleans alone. An even greater percentage of mixed marriages—perhaps as high as 10 percent—occurred in the North and West. Because large numbers of African Americans still had not migrated to these areas by the late 1890s, there were few members of their own race to meet and mingle with. As a result, the African Americans increasingly dated and married whites in the area. Among the prominent African-American leaders who married white women were Frederick Douglass and Archibald H. Grimké.

While some of these couples led quiet, harmonious lives, other interracial marriages were plagued by an array of problems. For example, Frederick Douglass's marriage to Helen Pitts produced a barrage of public criticism.

Dating and marriage patterns between African Americans and whites changed somewhat in the 1920s and 1930s. Hundreds of thousands of African Americans from the South who were subjected to segregation and mob lynchings there moved north, hoping to find better jobs and a less-repressive life-style. This migration later intensified during World War I (1914–1918), when foreign immigration was curtailed and workers were badly needed.

As Northern populations of African Americans rose, intermarriage declined, because African Americans increasingly married within their own race. African-American communities also solidified because whites found ways to restrict nonwhites from their social circles. Although African Americans and whites in the North and West still intermarried, the percentage of mixed marriages dropped to less than 1 percent. Nonetheless, there was still significantly more intermarriage in the North and West than in the South.

These interracial marriages usually involved middle-class couples. However, it was not uncommon for such interracial middle-class couples, as well as those less well off, to lose their jobs once either their supervisors or co-workers learned of their marriages. The couples also frequently found it difficult to buy a home or even rent an apartment.

White society, determined to prevent interracial romances or marriages, used a variety of obstacles. In one instance, a young white woman's grandmother had her committed to a mental institution after she announced her engagement to an African American. When Leroy Gardner, a young African American, entered Bethel College in St. Paul, Minnesota, in 1943, he had to sign a formal pledge, promising not to socialize with the white females on campus. He later married a white woman, although the bride's father had threatened to shoot him.

If a white woman married an African American, her friends and family might suggest that she was either immoral or unable to get a white husband. A divorced white woman who married an African American might lose custody of her children, since white judges often perceived these women as unfit mothers. Interracial couples also frequently contended with hate mail and obscene and threatening phone calls.

For the most part, celebrities who intermarried or interracial couples who were more affluent had an easier time. That was how it was for George and Josephine Schuyler, a racially mixed couple who married in 1928. Josephine, a white dancer and artist was the daughter of a Texas rancher. George, an African-American writer from New York, was a columnist for a popular periodical. They first met at the publication's editorial offices. During their courtship, they were frequently spotted at parties given by prominent African-American intellectuals as well as at fashionable New York night spots. The two later married and enjoyed an enduring relationship.

During World War II (1939–1945), a number of interracial marriages occurred between African-American servicemen and the white women they met overseas. African Americans who were regarded as war heroes in Europe hoped to be able to marry whomever they loved. But this frequently was not the case.

An African-American serviceman named Buford Simpkins learned this in 1942, when he became engaged to Hazel Byrne, a young white English woman. Simpkins was stationed in Hazel Byrne's hometown of Manchester, England, when he applied to his superior officer for permission to marry. Instead of receiving a few days' leave for the ceremony and honeymoon, Simpkins was transferred to another European base. Hazel Byrne suffered repercussions as a result of the engagement as well. Her family disowned her, and she was physically abused by a white serviceman who was opposed to her relationship with Simpkins.

Things improved somewhat for the couple as time passed. After a two-year delay and an intensive interview at the American embassy in London, Hazel Byrne was finally permitted to join her fiancé. The couple married and settled in Chicago after returning to the United States. The young woman was accepted by her in-laws but still faced harassment from both African-American and white men, who assumed she was a prostitute because she had married an African American.

Following the war, it was thought that African-American and white marriages would be more accepted. As African-American GIs returned home, the spirit of change was in the air. But while there were significant increases in interracial marriages in areas such as Washington, D.C., and New York, the national rate of mixed marriages between African Americans and whites rose less than 1 percent.

Race relations, with only a slight rise in intermarriage in some areas, did not change significantly until the 1960s. The civil rights movement of that decade, characterized by protest marches and demonstrations, dramatically altered the way African Americans and whites related to one another. African Americans, supported in their cause by sympathetic whites, became a potent force in American society. They mixed more easily in white circles, and perhaps for the first time in our nation's history, racially derogatory humor became unacceptable.

The legislation of this period also typified the overall feeling sweeping much of the country. Attempting to ensure racial equality, Congress passed the Civil Rights Act of 1964 and the Voting Rights Act of 1965. But the 1967 Supreme Court decision in the case of *Loving v. Commonwealth of Virginia* was especially relevant for those contemplating interracial marriage. With this decision, the Supreme Court invalidated state statutes banning mixed marriages.

These factors may have all played a part in the sharp increase in interracial dating and marriage at the time. Nearly twice as many African Americans and whites intermarried between 1960 and 1970 as had in the previous decade, and this trend continued. While there were 77,000 racially mixed weddings in the 1970s, this number climbed to 168,000 in the 1980s and continued to grow in the 1990s.

Despite the increase in mixed marriages, interracial dating and marriage became distinctly unfashionable in some African-American circles. The Black Power movement, which began in the 1960s and continued into the

1970s, stirred racial pride and underscored the importance of African Americans marrying African Americans. Speeches made by African-American leaders like Malcolm X and Stokely Carmichael about the values of black separatism and unity captured the minds of many African Americans. Although integration between African Americans and whites was still being encouraged by followers of Martin Luther King, Jr., others were asking African Americans to look to themselves for strength and fulfillment.

Attitudes changed, and by the 1980s a significant number of the barriers to interracial romance had broken down. With the Black Power movement softening as the previous decade drew to a close, some African-American spokespeople argued that it was possible to intermarry without risking racial identity and black pride. The essence of their philosophy was "Blacks are slowly learning that black is beautiful and that they need not feel inferior. Parents should not condemn black men in general because some marry white women. All men and women have the right to date and marry whomever they choose. This right should be respected."[1]

Liberalized attitudes toward black and white relationships became evident in the legal system as well. Many judges no longer felt that in awarding custody white children were automatically best off in all-white homes. This sentiment was incorporated into law in 1984 when the U.S. Supreme Court ruled out race as a factor in custody battles. In the determining case, the Court overturned a Florida court's decision denying a white woman custody of her six-year-old daughter because her second husband was African American.

1. Paul R. Spickard, *Mixed Blood: Intermarriage and Ethnic Identity in Twentieth-Century America* (Madison: University of Wisconsin Press, 1989), 305.

Some speculated that the increase in interracial dating and marriage was fostered by emerging social situations in which African Americans and whites mixed in new settings. While previously, whites and African Americans had interacted largely in a supervisor-worker capacity in the workplace, now many met as social equals on college campuses as well as on jobs.

Still another factor contributing to the increase in interracial dating and marriage may have been the existence of a growing African-American middle class. The children of the African-American middle class often grow up in largely white neighborhoods and, to a great extent, are somewhat isolated from significant numbers of African Americans.

These young African Americans attend mostly white schools, have white friends, and absorb the views and values of their white communities. As these individuals begin to date, many feel comfortable seeking white partners. Although some may consciously choose to date and marry other African Americans, many others find suitable white mates.

However, this phenomenon has hardly swept the nation. Despite the increase in African-American and white couples in recent years, the national percentage of intermarriages remains quite low. As of the early 1990s, only 3.6 percent of black men and 1.2 percent of black women had married someone of another race.

Interracial dating and marriage among other races in the United States warrant examination as well. The Asian-American experience may be of particular interest. Japanese immigration to the United States began in the 1860s with a sparse trickle of students, merchants, and others. In the next thirty years, Japanese immigration increased steadily, as companies recruited Japanese workers to come to the U.S. mainland and Hawaii. These men did not intend to stay but rather hoped to save a sum of money before returning home.

Japanese workers did not have an easy life in America. By the 1880s, anti-Chinese discrimination peaked in the United States; and as Asians, the few Japanese in this country were also routinely scorned. Anti-Chinese violence soon erupted throughout the West, resulting in a substantial loss of Asian life. Countless others were burned out of their homes. Since the Chinese continued to be viewed as a threat both to the jobs and to the values of whites, in 1882, Congress banned their further immigration to the United States. Many of the Chinese already here either returned to their homeland or retreated to newly evolving slum areas.

With the influx of cheap Chinese labor curtailed, newly arrived Japanese workers often took their places. But as many of the racist Asian stereotypes originally aimed at the Chinese were now applied to Japanese workers, a growing wave of anti-Japanese sentiment developed. Japanese immigrants frequently were falsely characterized as "sneaky," anxious to deprive Americans of employment opportunities, and unnaturally desirous of white women.

After the early 1900s, the nature of Japanese immigration changed somewhat. Despite the poor treatment they'd received, some of the men who originally came to the United States to work temporarily decided to remain here permanently. During this period, there was little intermingling between white women and Asian men. But to ensure that mixed marriages between the two races did not become commonplace, in 1905 the California assembly outlawed marriages between whites and Japanese. A leader of the all-white organization the National Daughters of the Golden West even issued the following warning to young white females. "It is not unusual these days to find especially the 'better class' of Japanese casting furtive glances at our young women. They would like to marry them."

Actually, most Japanese immigrants were not interested in marrying whites. Often the men went back to Japan to marry and returned to America shortly thereafter with their brides. Others asked their families in Japan to pick a suitable mate for them. After exchanging letters and photographs with the selected woman, the young man sent sufficient funds for her to come to America to marry him. This first generation of Japanese male and female immigrants was known as the *issei*.

The arrival of issei in the United States greatly changed Japanese-American life. The women brought all the comforts of home to the previously lonely men, and before long, issei communities developed on the West Coast. Some more-transient Japanese families settled in Montana, Texas, and New York, where there were few other Japanese. By the early 1920s, issei households existed in every state in the Union.

Over the years, Japanese-American families were forced to deal with discrimination on numerous levels. Hoping to keep out Asians, in 1924 Congress placed limits on immigration that nearly eliminated Japanese newcomers. But in spite of harassment, many issei remained in America. Their children, second-generation Japanese Americans, were referred to as the *nisei*.

To a great extent, nisei differed from their parents, who largely clung to traditional Japanese values. Nisei attended public schools and spent much of their spare time in non-Japanese-run stores or at amusement parks and playgrounds. Many admired the white American way of life and felt torn between their Japanese heritage and their desire for recognition and acceptance by their white peers. But nisei young people often found that regardless of how closely they conformed to white norms, they were not readily accepted. When white Americans looked at the nisei's complexions and heard their Japanese names, they tended to think of them as Asian rather than American.

Nisei children intermingled with whites throughout junior high school, but in high school and college, many were socially rejected. Japanese-American students who worked on school projects and in extracurricular clubs with whites generally were excluded from white dances and parties.

White Americans were not the only ones opposed to interracial mixing that might lead to marriage. The issei parents of nisei children were generally opposed to it as well. Intermarriage cast a stigma on the entire family, which the issei hoped to avoid at any cost. Many issei also felt that there were serious value differences between themselves and white Americans. They believed that whites did not take marriage seriously enough and were too quick to divorce.

In response, nisei formed their own social groups, which sponsored all-nisei dances, softball teams, picnics, and other outings. These groups contained almost no one who wasn't a nisei, but most of the young participants did not revert to the traditional Japanese values and customs of their parents. Instead, they persisted in dressing, speaking, and acting as "American" as possible.

Although most nisei dated one another, there were still some interracial romances. At times, nisei dated whites because they could not identify with their parents' prearranged marriages or had found individuals outside the Japanese-American community who wanted to be with them. There was also a greater degree of freedom in dating a white or Mexican American who did not have access to the gossip grapevines of their own closely knit Japanese-American communities. Nonetheless, only a fraction of nisei married whites, African Americans, or Hispanics.

Regardless of how American the native-born nisei might have felt, during World War II their own country turned against them. Shortly after the Japanese bombed Pearl Harbor in 1941, U.S. authorities forcibly removed all individuals of Japanese descent from their homes and placed them under guard in internment camps. This Asian roundup included Japanese Americans who, having been born in the United States, were American citizens. Many of these young people had never even seen Japan, but the government believed they still might be conspiring with the enemy.

Some sociologists think that their internment camp experiences contributed to the scant number of interracial nisei marriages during this period. In the camps, the nisei's contact with individuals of non-Japanese descent decreased greatly. Because they socialized exclusively with other Japanese Americans while confined, many young nisei became engaged to or married one another.

Their forced confinement was a shameful episode in American history. Still, most nisei refused to become demoralized. Although humiliated by their government, they declared their loyalty to the United States and valiantly strove to prove themselves worthy citizens. During the war, many young Japanese-American men joined the army once they were permitted to do so. The Japanese-American 442nd Regimental Combat Team adopted the motto Go for Broke and ranked among the most decorated units in American military history.

Once the conflict ended, nisei again embraced American society and its ideals. These Japanese Americans pursued educational opportunities with greater vigor than ever. Although by 1940 they had become America's most highly educated racial group, they were determined to reach new heights.

Throughout this period, many nisei exhibited a reaction that sociologists label "social amnesia." They tried to block out the painful memory of their World War II incarceration. Some nisei never told their children about the ordeal. Instead, most concentrated on securing a place for themselves in America's mainstream and getting their piece of the American dream.

In the decades following World War II, Japanese Americans moved to new areas of the country, and by the 1970s, many regions had a number of Japanese-American residents. While in the 1950s they had predominently clustered in urban ethnic communities, nisei now settled in suburbia as well.

In the 1960s, a new generation of Japanese Americans came of age. These were the *sansei*—the nisei's children who had been born shortly after the war. Like their parents, many sansei pursued advanced degrees and prestigious careers. However, these third-generation Japanese Americans intermingled with people of other races with greater ease than either their parents or grandparents had.

By the 1960s, Japanese Americans had already experienced a significant increase in interracial marriages. As early as 1967, 55 percent of the sansei who were seriously dating or engaged had chosen non-Japanese-American partners, and by 1972 that number had risen to 67 percent.

Sansei with non-Japanese-American spouses were usually less tied to their ethnic roots than those who married within their race. Fewer of them spoke Japanese, lived in heavily populated Japanese-American neighborhoods, or were members of Japanese cultural organizations. They were frequently well-educated individuals who had assimilated into the white middle-class world.

Nisei parents frequently had mixed reactions to these interracial marriages. Many accepted their offspring's white spouses, but some were adamantly opposed to their children marrying African Americans. This was a common source of contention, as a young sansei woman who loved an African-American man soon learned. Her experience was as follows. "Raised in a racially mixed neighborhood [Judy Ohashi] fell in love with an African-American high school classmate. Her parents, otherwise gracious people, were adamant in their desire not to meet the boy or his family. They forbade their daughter to continue seeing him. On graduation from high school, Ohashi briefly considered eloping with her boyfriend but could not break from her family. She gave him up. Fifteen years later she remained single and embittered against her parents, doting on the memory of her former lover."[2]

During the 1970s, a number of sansei became firmly opposed to any form of interracial dating. Many of these individuals were students involved in the Asian Power movement on college campuses. Young Asian Americans—primarily Chinese, Japanese, and Filipinos—had banded together to protest the negative stereotypes and discrimination endured by their peoples. These activists fought for an Asian studies curriculum and an enhanced general awareness and appreciation of Asian culture.

---

2. Ibid., 67.

The Asian Power movement also influenced expectations about social relationships and prospective marriage partners. The young activists discouraged interracial romances, especially with whites. They stressed the importance of Asians dating one another, arguing that people of European descent could never truly understand the Asian experience. Not all sansei agreed with this perception. Many continued to date and marry individuals they cared for, regardless of that person's race.

We have explored the dating and interracial marriage experiences of two American minorities: African Americans and Japanese Americans. Yet there are numerous other minorities—among them Middle Easterners, Filipinos, and Chinese—who have intermingled with others of differing backgrounds to help form our national heritage. Hispanics have a history in America dating back to the conquistadores; and, more recently, we have witnessed an influx of new immigrants from Vietnam, Cambodia, and Laos.

It is not possible to trace the romantic experiences of every group. However, through interviews with a variety of people for this book, we have provided a view of what it is like to date or marry someone whose racial or ethnic background differs from your own. Both the teenagers and adults featured here point to both the possible benefits and drawbacks inherent in their choices. They all speak from the heart, offering their personal perspectives. Without realizing it, they may already be weaving the newest addition to the multicultural tapestry of American life.

PART ONE

The Teenagers Speak

ONE

Christopher Gregory Sorhaindo

"I'm a high school senior, and last year I dated a white girl for the first time. She was in one of my classes at school. Montclair [New Jersey] is supposed to be fairly well integrated, but, in a way, my school is segregated. The high school has three class levels: advanced placement, honors level, and the regular classes. I take advanced placement courses, and there aren't many other African Americans in my classes—especially males. Quite a few smart black kids come from families that can't afford to give them the same advantages as white households.

"My parents are from the Dominican Republic, where the old-fashioned work ethic was instilled in them. I was brought up the same way. I'm extremely ambitious. I've got so much drive that my friends say I'm

19

hyper. I get good grades, have a part-time job at the library, and am taking flying lessons to get my pilot's license.

"A friend introduced me to my white girlfriend. I can't say exactly what attracted us to each other. But she was smart and good-looking, and we liked being together. We were friends for about a year before things got romantic.

"My black friends don't date people of other races. In a way, I was trying to break down that barrier, but they think that's impossible. They call interracial dating 'going across the border'; and when I started seeing the white girl, they kept saying, 'What's the sense?'

"I wasn't put off by our racial differences because my family is racially mixed. My great-grandfather was Italian, and my grandfather was British and Indian. My parents never expressed any particular preference as to the race of the girls I dated.

"But that didn't stop my friends from teasing me about having a white girlfriend. Some of them are firmly opposed to interracial mixing. I asked several African-American girls how they felt about it, and they said they wouldn't go out with a white boy under any circumstances. They don't want to deal with the prejudice they'll come up against.

"It's also extremely important to them to keep the black race black. I know a girl whose parents have a mixed marriage, and when I asked her how she feels about it, she said that sometimes she feels white and other times she feels black. Some African-American girls don't want to date white boys because if it leads to marriage, their kids might suffer. Children can be very cruel in these situations. A few black girls I know might consider having white boyfriends, but they'd make sure that these relationships didn't go any further.

"I never brought my white girlfriend to parties where my black friends were. They always made a point of introducing me to different black girls. I never pursued these young women since, at the time, I was only interested in the white girl I was seeing.

"I can't say the white girls are better than black girls, but it was easier to be with my girlfriend than with many of the African-American girls I dated. Black girls can be bossy and demanding. Sometimes they 'dog us,' acting as if they're the center of the universe and we're there to please them. When a black girl wants something, she expects to get it.

"Black women develop strength and independence as survival skills. With a large proportion of black men either on drugs or in jail, many African-American women head households. They've had to be both mother and father to their children. I understand what they're up against, but that doesn't necessarily make them fun to date. I've seen some of my black friends get bossed around by their girlfriends. These girls see how their mothers are and act the same way.

"In our household, my mother's in control. She runs things even though my father has always lived with us and holds down a job. I have a sister who tries to dominate me, but I fight her on it—I have a mind of my own. Maybe African-American women feel they have to be in charge, but they could be pushing away the black men headed for success, who also want to feel capable.

"I think some black women don't even realize how they come across. African-American females have never lived in our society free of subjugation. But as the women try to prove that they're finally fully emancipated, the black man may just happen to be in the way.

"My white girlfriend treated me as an equal, and that's important to me. She had a soft quality about her and was more considerate than most of the African-American girls I'd been with. I think that white girls are usually less angry than black girls. Maybe it's easy for them to be that way since they don't have the concerns black women face.

"I'm not like the average black guy who's trying to live up to a streetwise stereotype. I want to succeed. I've been called an Oreo [black on the outside, white inside]. That label is unfair because I've put up with as much racism as anybody else—sometimes more. I'm up for the Boy Scouts' Eagle rank. Not many blacks make it to that level, it's considerably harder for a black than a white.

"I've never been readily accepted by whites. Instead, I've become painfully aware of how racism keeps me and other African Americans on the sidelines. Even white students who admire my academic ability are conscious of our racial differences. They'll say, 'He's a brain,' but they don't want to socialize with me. I'm not with my white girlfriend anymore, and I'm not sure whether or not race was a factor in our breakup. I only know that she began dating a white guy shortly afterward.

"You can't deny that prejudice and discrimination exist. I have one African-American friend who thinks she's too light skinned and another who feels he's too dark. The whole emphasis on color and status is very complex. White people go to tanning salons or bake for hours in the hot sun to darken themselves, yet black people still can't take their rightful place in society.

"I don't see racism disappearing anytime soon. I think the bigotry would only end if everyone intermarried and had children. If we were all the same color, no one could be hated because of his or her complexion."

TWO

Peta-Anne Jones

"I was born in Jamaica, where there're a number of dif-
ferent ethnic groups. Most Americans think that all Jamaicans are black, but that isn't so. There are Indians,
whites, and others besides the blacks there. My mother
was born in Jamaica, and she's half Chinese.

"Racism is not a factor on the island. If a black person and a white person get together, they're identified
as Jamaicans, not by their race. People in Jamaica are
more aware of class distinctions, which are usually determined by financial status.

"I didn't know about racism until I came to the
United States at age seven. I had a crush on a white boy
in the fourth grade. When we were in the sixth grade, I
found out that he liked me, too. But by then it was too

late, I didn't like him anymore. My friends and I really became interested in boys when we were about twelve or thirteen. I liked a handsome black boy named Doug. We dated from the seventh through the ninth grades.

"While growing up, I lived in a black neighborhood in Morristown [New Jersey]. Many of the teenagers there were angry, and strong antiwhite feelings were common. They had a street they called the Holler or something like that. If a white person drove down that street, they'd stone the car.

"The black girls I hung out with in high school had a definite attitude problem. They made a point of not socializing with or even talking to white people. I never once saw a black girl date a white boy the whole time I was with them. That wasn't a problem for me, because I wasn't attracted to any of the white boys I saw in Morristown. I also hadn't felt drawn to the local Indian or Asian boys.

"Some of the black Morristown girls dated both black and Hispanic boys. Several of these guys were light skinned and had white features. While the same girls wouldn't be caught dead with a white boy, they wanted to date the Hispanics. Some of the boys dressed like black guys, but the girls even went for the ones who didn't. I think they just considered Hispanics on their level and felt comfortable with them.

"Morristown black girls may not have gone out with white boys, but some of the black guys dated white girls. That was supposed to be okay, and it annoyed me. A black guy who went out with a white girl was seen as a stud. But if a black girl ever dated a white, people would say that she wanted to be white. The boy she went out with might also be beaten up, either while he was with her or afterward.

"The high school blacks who dated white girls were usually school sports stars. Their ability on the court or field made them minicelebrities, and the white kids wanted to be with them. Sometimes when I saw good-looking black boys with white girls who weren't very attractive, I wondered if they were going out with them just because they were white.

"In some ways, leaving Morristown for Parsippany changed the way I felt and acted. Parsippany is more racially mixed, and although there are more white than black people here, I haven't encountered much racism. Morristown's racial tensions would have stopped me from dating a white, but I can see myself going out with a white boy here if I met someone I liked. My parents wouldn't care. In discussing it with my mother, she said that a man's color isn't as important as how he treats you.

"It isn't an issue for me now that I'm in college, because I've been with a black guy named Derrick for the past two and a half years. I don't think I'd have bothered with Derrick if I still had my Morristown mentality. I probably would have thought that he was trying to be white. The minute I saw him I knew he was no 'home boy.' He had a conservative haircut, a preppy outfit, and there wasn't a single 'yo' in his conversation.

"Derrick's family is from Jamaica, like mine. He's black, but he always dated white girls before we started going together. That was because of where he lives. Derrick's is one of four black families in the affluent New Jersey town of Franklin Lakes. When Derrick was in high school, there weren't any black girls around for him to go out with. We were introduced by a mutual friend from another town.

"I started college this fall, and I guess that if I still lived in Morristown, my old friends would say that I was trying to be white. Not many of those girls planned on going to college. A few already have their own babies.

"I visited Morristown a while ago, but there was nothing there for me anymore. I've had a chance to think things through, and I'm my own person now. I've made new friends—my circle isn't all black anymore. My three best girlfriends are Egyptian, Pakistani, and Chinese.

"If Derrick and I marry, we'll probably live in a town that's more racially mixed than Franklin Lakes. But no matter where or how well a black person lives in America, it's impossible to entirely escape racism.

"A good example of this occurred one afternoon when my boyfriend was out riding in his new Corvette. As he leaned forward to change the radio station, Derrick accidentally went through a stop sign. Moments later he was stopped by a police officer. Derrick was sure he'd get a ticket; but instead, the officer asked my boyfriend, 'How'd you get enough money for a car like that?'

"Derrick told him that he was just hardworking. The officer warned him to drive carefully and sent Derrick on his way. It wasn't the type of special treatment anyone would really want. Can you imagine the police stopping a white man in a Corvette to ask him how he got the money to pay for the car?"

THREE

Ai-De Chang

"I was born in Taiwan and came to this country as a teenager with my family in May 1990. Chinese people are very conservative. My parents did not let me date in Taiwan; they wanted me to concentrate on my studies. Most Taiwanese parents feel as they do. Although some teenage girls are allowed to go out with boys, many who date do so secretly, hoping that their parents and teachers never find out.

"When we came to the United States, my mother and father still didn't want me to go out with boys. At first, I obeyed them; but after I saw how many American girls had boyfriends, I wanted one, too. I knew that if I found a boyfriend, my parents could never know about it.

"One boy I went out with came to America from

Taiwan about six years ago. He had definitely become more American than Chinese. He wore jeans, T-shirts, and jewelry. He even had an earring in one ear. In Taiwan, respectable boys wear suits and always look refined. If my boyfriend went to Taiwan looking as he does, people there would think he was immoral.

"My boyfriend also didn't act like a typical Chinese boy. He reminded me of the Hispanics at school. He's very outgoing and would think nothing of kissing a girl on the cheek at school. A boy in Taiwan would never do that unless the girl was his girlfriend. Even then he probably wouldn't hug or kiss her at school.

"At first, I didn't like this almost-American boy from my country. I thought of him as a flirtatious playboy. I knew that he liked another girl who didn't feel the same way about him, but I couldn't see us as a couple. During this time, I had begun to date a boy from Korea. He recently came to this country, and I guess I felt comfortable with him because we were both Asian and I knew that he liked me.

"But there were some things about my Korean boyfriend that I didn't like. He was very domineering; and when I discussed this with my Korean girlfriend, she told me that in their country, a Korean man can slap his wife if she angers him. Maybe some Korean women will put up with this kind of behavior, but I knew that I never could.

"Since the Korean boy had only just come to America, neither of us spoke English very well. If I spent most of my time around people who didn't know the language I needed to learn, I wondered how I was ever going to become fluent in English.

"Meanwhile, my feelings about the Taiwanese boy changed as I learned more about him. I realized that maybe he wasn't really a playboy but just liked being around people. When he went to visit his relatives in Taiwan for the summer, I missed him. After he returned to school in the fall, he told one of my girlfriends that he liked me.

"I had to decide whether I was going to be with him or the Korean boy I'd spent the summer with. I knew that I didn't love my Korean boyfriend. I also felt that he'd gotten used to me and had begun to take our relationship for granted. I decided to break off with him.

"I started seeing the Taiwanese boy, and before long I fell in love with him. It wasn't hard. He was handsome, charming, and spoke English beautifully. He became very important to me, and that's why I tried to get him to change the way he dressed and acted around people. Having been brought up in Taiwan, I thought his clothes were too casual. I could never introduce him to my parents if he came to dinner wearing jeans and an earring. I'd also kept telling him not to be so wild. I never wanted to hurt him. I only tried to change him because he meant so much to me.

"As all this was happening, my Taiwanese boyfriend got friendly with a blond, blue-eyed girl from school. He complained to her about how I couldn't accept him as he was. She told him that she thought he was perfect and that I was lucky to have him. When I asked him about her, he said that they were just friends and that he wasn't interested in her romantically.

"He lied. While we were going out together, that girl gave him a silver ring. When I asked him about it, he said the ring was a gift from his mother. I also later learned that he'd been with the blond girl when he told me he was somewhere else.

"I thought that girl might damage our relationship,

so when we returned to school after Christmas vacation, I decided to speak to her. I told her that I was sorry if what I said hurt her but that she'd already hurt me by giving my boyfriend a ring and interfering in our relationship.

"Our talk didn't help things. My boyfriend broke up with me in January. He said that he wanted more freedom than I could give him. I loved him but had pushed too hard for him to be like the boys I admired in Taiwan. I wanted him to fit into a culture I felt comfortable with but that he had left behind.

"Being without him was awful. Almost as soon as he left, I knew that the problem was mine, not his. If you live in a country, you should be free to adopt its ways. If he were willing to come back, I'd work on changing myself and accept him as he is. I learned too late that a person is always more important than customs and clothing."

FOUR

Waldir Sepulveda

"I was born in Colombia and lived there as a boy with my family. We had an apartment in a big city that was like New York. But other things in Colombia were very different than they are in the States.

"Dating is much more serious there. In America, you might casually ask a girl out and just go to the beach or a movie. But in Colombia, first you have to tell a girl that you're interested in her and that you want to see her. Even if she wants to be with you, a couple still can't go out right away. Her parents have to trust you. That means that you'll be spending time at her house while her family's there.

"Once they feel that they know you, you may be allowed to take her to the movies. Some families are very strict, and you're expected to always show your respect for them. So things go considerably slower than in America.

"When I was about twelve years old, my family came to New York. I went to a special bilingual school. There were kids there from several Spanish-speaking countries, but hardly any Colombian girls. The few there had already become very Americanized and were really aggressive in how they'd come on to you. I was very shy and kept thinking how in Colombia it was up to the boy to make the first move.

"The American girls were even worse. My bilingual classes were on the fourth floor, and when I went down to the third and second floors for the other periods, I'd meet them there. They ran after boys in the hall and embraced them whenever they said hello or good-bye. I'd attended a very strict Catholic school in Colombia, and it seemed as if these girls were going against everything I'd ever learned.

"Things really worsened when this Dominican guy at the school and some of his friends ganged up on me because the girl he liked was after me. Luckily, it didn't go any further because the girl threatened to kick his butt if he didn't call it off. I know it sounds funny, but, at the time, it seemed as if this tough girl actually saved my life.

"After a while, I got the hang of things. When I was fourteen, I dated an eighteen-year-old girl who was also from Colombia. I didn't feel our age difference was a problem, since I was used to being around adults and she and I got along well. Of course, my friends couldn't resist teasing her about going out with someone so much younger. They used to laugh and call her my baby-sitter.

"At sixteen, I started going out with girls who weren't from Colombia. By then I was attending an international school that had students from around the world.

I was especially interested in a Polish girl I'd been watching from a distance. I had a female Russian friend and asked her advice on the best way to approach the pretty Polish student.

"I thought that she was on my side, but she tried to talk me out of it. She said that the girl I liked came from a very small town in Poland and could hardly speak English. When she saw that she hadn't discouraged me, she added that the Polish girl was really stupid. She also accused me of just wanting to date the girl because she was good-looking. My Russian friend suggested that she and I go out together instead, but I told her it would spoil our friendship.

"I realized that the Russian girl wasn't going to help me meet the girl I liked, but after a while, a mutual friend of mine and the Polish girl introduced us. I was surprised to find that her English wasn't bad at all. We didn't go out at first, but instead just talked.

"I finally told her that I'd liked her from the moment I saw her and had said to myself that she was going to be my girlfriend. Then I felt embarrassed, thinking that I'd told her too much. So I lied and said that now I realized that it would be best if we were just friends. I was hoping she'd disagree, because I still wanted to go out with her. But she seemed content with a friendship.

"Surprisingly, the Russian girl came to my assistance. She asked the Polish girl if she'd ever date me. When I heard that she said yes, I finally asked her out. But we didn't have a problem-free romance. I found it hard to discuss my feelings with her. She just didn't want to talk about anything personal or meaningful. I'd tell her that I was mad enough at someone to kill him, and she'd say something like 'Hey, did you ever notice that I'm taller than you?'

"I think she'd do anything to avoid a deep conversation. I discussed this with her, but she said that's the way she's always been and she can't help it. She added, 'What do you expect of me? I'm not Hispanic.'

"Her family is among the few white families in a neighborhood of mostly Puerto Ricans and Dominicans. Her father hates Hispanics. At first, his daughter felt the same way. But once she started school in America, she met lots of us and saw that we're all individuals, just like anyone else. Her father still doesn't know what we're really like and doesn't want to know.

"My girlfriend's father also doesn't know that I'm from Colombia. She and her friend concocted a story to make me more acceptable to him. They told him that I'm from Spain and that my skin is just a shade darker than theirs. Being European instead of Colombian was supposed to have made me more desirable in his estimation. I guess it wasn't in the Polish rule book for me to be accepted for who I am. I still haven't met her father, although he's heard quite a bit about me. I doubt that very much of it is true though.

"I still have several Colombian friends. We were close for years since we all started at the international school at about the same time. I've benefited from making friends with people from other countries, but my Hispanic friends don't want to mix with whites. At school, they hang out together in their own group. You'll usually find them in the corner by the bathroom. The problem is that you don't learn anything by excluding everyone who's not like you. They're still talking about the same things they discussed two years ago.

"While they're in the corner, most of the white kids hang out in the school's lounge. Lately, I've spent time in the lounge, and my Colombian friends have accused me of turning my back on them. There's a commercial on a

Spanish cable television channel in which a Hispanic man advertising an English course tells viewers, 'Follow me into the world of English.' Now whenever my Colombian friends see me in the lounge, they call me 'Follow Me.'

"My Hispanic friends don't like white girls. They say that they're conceited, can't cook, and are too stuck-up. When I first came to the States, even my sister had some nasty things to say about Americans. She told me that they never washed their sneakers and that they only ate hamburgers from McDonald's. It was as if you said all Mexicans only eat tacos.

"Now I feel like I'm between two worlds. I'm still close to a few Hispanics, who feel as I do and want to break away from the pack. But when I pass by my old group while holding hands with my Polish girlfriend, she feels uncomfortable. I'm always afraid that they'll say something. They've never said anything in front of her but later on have asked me why I always hang out with white girls. They'll say, 'Don't you know that whites think they're better than us?'

"There's a popular Hispanic girl who used to like me, but now she hates my guts. She thinks Hispanic boys shouldn't date whites. Sometimes when I'm with my Hispanic friends, she'll ask where my white girlfriend is.

"It gets hard for me. If I go to the lounge to hang out with the white kids, I don't completely fit in there either. So I go back and forth between both groups. I've become a sort of nomad."

FIVE

Lily Leon

"My family is Chinese, but I was born and raised in Peru before coming to the United States. Years ago when the Japanese invaded China, my grandfather fled to Peru and started a business there. Before long my grandmother followed with their five children. That's how my mother, aunts, and uncle grew up in Peru. We weren't the only Asian family either. There were quite a few others, and we even had our own Chinatown. My mother met my father, who was also Chinese, in Peru. They married, and later on I was born.

"We left Peru four years ago, when I was twelve. Although I didn't date before coming to America, I know that Peruvian young people get to know each other well before they start going out.

"In America, girls go out with lots of different guys. I began dating when I was about fourteen or fifteen. All the boys I've gone out with are Hispanic. Maybe that's just a coincidence, but I like those boys and feel at home with them. My parents may be Chinese, but I grew up in a Spanish-speaking country. My mother understands that I'm attracted to Hispanic boys, but she'd rather I dated someone Chinese. I guess that way he wouldn't feel lost if he came to our home for dinner.

"My mother tolerates my Hispanic boyfriends now, but she'll really be mad if I don't marry a Chinese boy. When she says Chinese, she means Asians in general. Asians are more reserved than Hispanics. You never see them running through the halls at school or yelling out to their friends. When I'm with Asian kids, I act more conservatively, and my mother knows it.

"My grandmother wouldn't like it either if I didn't marry a Chinese person. Two of my uncles married Hispanic women, and she doesn't feel right around their wives. I think that the ideal guy for me would be an Asian boy who acts like a Hispanic. I wish someone like that existed. He'd understand exactly how I think.

"Sometimes I feel torn between being Chinese and being Hispanic. I speak Spanish and have quite a few Hispanic friends that I really like. But when I'm at home with my family, I feel more Chinese. This mixture can be a problem when I first meet people. I speak very little Chinese, and they're always surprised when they hear me speak fluent Spanish because I don't look Hispanic. I look Chinese. Of course, there are some benefits to blending into two cultures. I like traveling in both circles. Whether I go to a Hispanic dance or a Chinese gathering, I always feel comfortable.

"I hang out with both Hispanic and Chinese kids.

But my Chinese and Hispanic friends stay in their separate groups and don't mingle with one another. They're really very different. The Chinese kids are usually more influenced by their parents and study more. Often both the Hispanic parents work, so they don't spend as much time with their children. They're less demanding about school and grades than Chinese parents are.

"I love Spanish music and would like to live in a Hispanic community, because these neighborhoods tend to be more alive than the quiet residential areas I've lived in with my family. Yet in some ways, I lean toward Asian values. School is really important to me because I know that's the only way to get anywhere. My family is poor, but they've tried to give me everything. I want to go to college so I can give something back to them.

"I guess there's an advantage to dating and marrying someone of your own race and culture. But in so many ways, I feel both Chinese and Hispanic. If I ever learned to cook, I don't know if I'd want to prepare Spanish or Chinese food. And if I had to choose one culture over the other, I don't know which I'd pick."

SIX

Eve Kaplan

"I was a student in a private school in New York City when I first met Charlie. I'm Jewish, my mother is a doctor, and my father's in the stock market—but Charlie's background is different. He's Vietnamese and had arrived in America as a consequence of the Vietnam War. Actually, that conflict seemed to have changed his life forever. Charlie was originally from a wealthy family somewhere in the country's north. His parents weren't political, they just wanted to leave Vietnam to ensure the safety of their five children. Fortunately, they had enough money to go to America, but they had to leave everything behind. So in coming to the United States, Charlie's family went from being upper middle class to middle class or lower middle class.

"Charlie was the first person of another race I'd ever dated. But there really wasn't anything extraordinary about our going out, because there was a lot of interracial dating at our school. I have friends who date people of other races and backgrounds, and most of them don't even consider these factors in deciding who to go out with. There were assemblies at school dealing with various aspects of multicultural mixing. Afterward, Charlie and I would discuss how we differed, but we decided that people are more the same than they are different.

"I'd known Charlie for a while before we went out. We met during our freshman year of high school—I used to see him a lot because our lockers were near each other. Sometimes we hung out together, but that was the extent of it. Then I didn't see very much of him since I was going with someone else during my sophomore year. After that we seemed to run into each other all the time. We flirted a lot, and both of us knew that we wanted to go out; but Charlie was too shy to ask me. So I asked him instead.

"I was the first girl Charlie ever dated, and when he brought me home to meet his family, they were really nice to me. His mother was hospitable and always cooked dinner for us. But the language barrier prevented the two of us from ever becoming really close. Her English was extremely limited, and Charlie had to act as our translator. Still, she'd make a point of smiling and saying Hi to me. I never saw that much of Charlie's father, since he worked long hours and was rarely home when I was there.

"Maybe Charlie's parents didn't oppose our relationship because he was their youngest child and they'd already been through this with their older children. I knew Charlie's mother and father were more protective of his sisters, but all Charlie's siblings were very Americanized.

Two of them went to Cornell, and I think the other two went to the University of Rochester. One of his sisters had been dating a blond white boy.

"But even though his parents accepted me and allowed his brothers and sisters to make their own dating choices, Charlie still had to contend with more restrictions than the average American boy his age. He told me that his parents didn't like him staying over at a friend's home, going out too much, or even staying out late.

"You hear so much about racism, but as far as I know, Charlie didn't experience a lot of it. He lived in a very racially mixed neighborhood of the Bronx [a borough of New York City], and was a good athlete. To a great extent, I think his sports ability helped him win social acceptance. He always dressed like any typical American boy and just seemed to fit in.

"Of course, Charlie had an accent and must have been aware of the small number of Asian students at our elite private school, but he didn't appear bothered by it. My Vietnamese boyfriend also often defied the stereotypes associated with Asians. He did all right in math but certainly wasn't a math whiz, the way people expect Asians to be.

"Another reason why Charlie may have seemed so American was that he really wasn't into Asian culture. Although he was Buddhist and his mother was teaching him to write Chinese, Charlie didn't have a firm sense of his ethnic identity. I remember telling him that he should know more about his heritage, but he wasn't interested in pursuing it, and I respected his feelings.

"I can't say that there were any real cultural barriers between us. I was only sharply aware of our differences on rare occasions, like the first time I noticed a small altar on the floor of his parents' home. The altar's interior was covered with a decorative fabric, and there were candles in it as well. Although I knew it was a religious altar, I wasn't sure of precisely what it was for. Charlie wasn't very religious, but his family celebrated the Chinese New Year and some other holidays.

"Yet I wasn't usually conscious of our differences unless someone said something negative about us. That's what happened the summer I was dating Charlie when I went backpacking with some friends. I wrote to Charlie from our campsite, and a boy noticed his name on the envelope. With a bewildered look on his face, he asked, 'What is he—Chinese?' One of the boys in the group was really surprised that I was dating Charlie. That's what sometimes makes interracial dating difficult. When people learn about your relationship, there's always this awkward pause in the conversation. It's embarrassing; it's like they're shocked or something.

"My backpacking buddies teased me about dating Charlie. The girls in the group didn't say much, but the boys couldn't understand why a white girl would go out with an Asian or anyone of another race, for that matter. They made it clear that they didn't find people of other races physically attractive.

"In some ways, things were easier with my family. Even before we'd started dating, my parents had known Charlie from school. My mother was supportive of my decision to go out with him. She commented on his good looks, and that made me feel good. My father seemed a little less comfortable with it, but it was still okay. The only strong objections came from my grandmother.

"She wanted to know who I was going out with, and as soon as I told her his name, she asked about Charlie's nationality. My grandmother found it really difficult to accept that he was of Chinese-Vietnamese extraction, and we argued about it. She said that Jewish people should stick with their own kind. My grandmother lives in the

Midwest in a very homogeneous community and that may account for her feelings. I even had Charlie meet her so that my grandmother could see what he was like, but she was still upset about our relationship.

"My grandmother knew that I'd dated Jewish boys in the past, and she'd been brought up to believe that was the way it was supposed to be. Her mother was an immigrant and had learned firsthand how difficult things could be if you were ethnically different. But my parents are Jewish and pretty liberal, and I grew up with a broader view of things. In speaking to other young people with similar experiences, I also noticed that parents are generally more apt to accept interracial or intercultural dating than grandparents.

"I think the couple's age is a factor in these relationships as well, since many people find interracial dating more acceptable than mixed marriages. I'm not going to marry Charlie, we broke up after about five months. But we didn't break up because we were an interracial couple. Things just became less intense as time passed, and I guess I began to lose interest. I started dating another boy about three weeks after our breakup. His father is a nonpracticing Jew, and I think his mother is Irish.

"I graduated from high school and am going to Harvard in the fall. Both my parents are Harvard graduates, and I'm really excited about being there. Harvard is very ethnically diverse, and I'll probably be dating people of other cultures and races. I want to be open to new experiences.

"When I have my own children, I'd certainly allow them to date a variety of people but would caution them about the difficulties associated with mixed marriages. Yet I still feel that if two people love each other and are close, their relationship can thrive regardless of their differences."

SEVEN

Roger Silva

"I was born in Brazil and lived there as a young child. I stayed with my grandparents since my parents were divorced and my mother's modeling career kept her on the road. We came to America when I was thirteen.

"Things were different here. There were almost daily fights among the kids at my new school. I didn't expect American teenagers to be so violent. It was quieter where I lived in Brazil.

"Dating is different in America, too. In Brazil, relationships usually last longer and are more honest. You develop a friendship with the person you're seeing. You don't just jump into something with someone you hardly know. But in the United States, you meet a girl at a dance, date her, and before you know it, you're not with that person anymore.

"The first girl I dated in America came here from Colombia. After we started going out together, I knew it wasn't going to last. We didn't have very much in common. She was extremely religious and not too open to new ideas. Our goals and interests never seemed to match. When I was with her, I knew that I shouldn't be. Our relationship ended in about a month.

"The next girl I went out with was Chinese. I'd met her while I was dating the Colombian girl, and we became good friends. We began spending more time together, and after a while, we started dating. We were very close. Sometimes it felt like we were thinking the same thoughts.

"My family liked my girlfriend, and I got along well with her family. She lived with her mother and sister, and I spent a lot of time at her house. I was accepted there, they treated me like a son.

"My girlfriend and I dated for over a year. We spent nearly all our free time together. Now I think that perhaps we were too close. We didn't give each other much breathing space, so often other activities had to be pushed aside. We used to fight over my taking time for my acting. I want to be a professional actor, and since I've been in high school, I've auditioned for and won roles in several school plays.

"My girlfriend resented the time I took to learn my lines and attend rehearsals. She used to say that I needed twenty-four hours a day for my acting and insisted that I give it up. She felt that it hurt us as a couple.

"I didn't want to stop acting, and my girlfriend and I continually fought about it. The disagreements led to our breakup. Shortly afterward, I was involved in an automobile accident and landed in the hospital for two weeks. When my former girlfriend came to visit me every day, I was moved by her kindness. It made me remember all the good things about her. We tried going out again after I felt better, but it just didn't work out between us. Cultural differences might have been a factor in my breakup with the Colombian girl, but my second girlfriend and I just grew apart as people.

"Lately, I've begun dating an American girl. I may live in America, but I still think of myself as Brazilian. I don't know yet if there'll be cultural differences between us, because the relationship is still too new. In deciding whether to ask out an American girl or one from Brazil, the country she came from would not be a determining factor. I'd be more interested in what type of person she was.

"Relationships with people who are different from us are not necessarily troublesome, although I think my grandparents would object if I brought home a black girl. But if I were forced to choose between my grandparents and a black girl I loved, I'd pick the girl. She would be the most important thing to me, and I think my grandparents would eventually come around.

"People should be with whomever they want as long as there's trust and affection in their relationships. You can't be afraid of what your family will say. It's better to try to talk to them so that there's a possibility of working things out. In the end, only you can determine who you'll love and want to be with."

EIGHT

Lynna Seow

"I'm sixteen years old and came here two and a half years ago from Malaysia. My first boyfriend in the United States was an African American whose real name is David, but everybody calls him Rock 'n' Roll because of the music he likes. I met Rock 'n' Roll when my girlfriend and I went to a program at a youth center. I was wearing sneakers, which I'd covered with slogans about peace and ecology, such as Save the Gorillas. I saw David looking at my feet, and when he realized that I'd noticed him, he told me that my shoes were cool.

"At first I wasn't very impressed. I thought, 'Here's another guy bugging me about my feet who's going to ask me for my phone number.' But it didn't happen that way. My friend introduced us, and we talked for a long time.

He wanted to know all about me and asked quite a few questions. That brought us closer. Even though he was really shy, he managed to tell me that he liked me.

"He seemed nice, but I didn't want a relationship just then. I mainly wanted to study, because getting into college was very important to me.

"There were other things to think about, too. Coming from Malaysia, my values differ from those of many American teenagers. I don't believe in premarital sex. Kissing and hugging are okay, but nothing more. I grew up with these beliefs, and they're important to me. I know that a lot of guys won't accept my value system, but I can't compromise on that.

"David turned out to be unusual. He kept trying to convince me to go out with him. It took a long time, but he never lost interest in me or the hope that we could work out our differences. He said that he respected my values but that he still wanted to go out with me. David was sweet and understanding, and I decided to take a chance.

"At first, I wasn't very attracted to him, but that didn't matter. I was more interested in his character. Besides, David became more attractive to me as we continued to date.

"At times, our different backgrounds made things awkward. David's mother was very nice to me whenever I went to their home, but I didn't know what to call her. I'd been brought up to respect my elders, and in Malaysia you show that respect by calling all adults close to you Auntie or Uncle. I asked David how to address his mother, and he told me to call her Mom. I didn't feel right doing that either. So I avoided calling her by name, and whenever I saw her, I just was friendly.

"David's family liked me. I'd told them about my

goals for the future—that I want to be an animal ecologist and do fieldwork. When I was accepted to Vanderbilt College in Tennessee, they were really excited and happy for me. Rock 'n' Roll had brought girls home before, but his other relationships didn't last very long. I knew that I was different: I was quieter and more disciplined. They were Americans, and I was a traditional Malaysian girl.

"At first, my mother was very upset about my being with David. It had nothing to do with his race. She didn't care about his skin color; she was just worried about my having a boyfriend at my age. She went into this big thing about how we were only in this country a short time and that we really didn't know these people.

"My mother was trying to shelter me from Americans. It's important to her that I keep our Malaysian values and not be influenced by outsiders. She thinks that the United States is a good place to work and live, but she isn't very impressed with the personal lives of Americans.

"In Malaysia, there's a lot of close bonding among relatives and friends. We lived with my grandmother until I was five years old. When we finally left, we only moved across the street. I still saw my grandmother every day. Malaysian families make a point of living near their relatives. That's not always so in America.

"Undoubtedly, there are differences between David and me. He likes American food and rarely eats Asian dishes. He usually has hot dogs, hamburgers, and waffles. When I asked him to try some food from my country, he said, 'That stuff looks green. I can't eat it.' Our tastes in music also differ. I like all kinds of music, including rock 'n' roll. But when I ask David to listen to something he's not familiar with, he tells me to put on rock 'n' roll instead.

"Even though David isn't always willing to try what I like, I've profited from being around him and his friends and family. You learn something from every new experience, whether it's good or bad. It helps you to decide whether you should change what you're doing or continue on as you have been. It's part of an evaluation process that's important both in dating and in life.

"I haven't always been pleased with David's evaluation of me, but I guess that can't be helped. Once when I was trying to get him to do something, he turned to me and said, 'You know, Lynna, you're very demanding.' Hearing that hurt, and I quickly denied that I was. But after thinking about it, I had to admit that there was some truth in what David said.

"But being demanding or having high standards isn't always negative. I think it reflects the Malaysian culture I love. In my country, you're brought up to expect both more of yourself and others. Students tend to be more disciplined about their work and take their assignments seriously.

"We also learn much more about other nations. When I was very small, I already knew all about the United States and many other countries throughout the world. But young American students don't know about Malaysia or a lot of other places for that matter. In a way, Americans are conceited. They think their country is the most important place on earth and that other people aren't as important. Sometimes that attitude also comes through in relationships with them.

"As the school year came to a close, I told David that I needed some space before leaving for Vanderbilt this fall. I said that for a little while I didn't want to think about pleasing him or my mother. I just wanted to be on my own.

"I care about David, and when someone means that much to me, I worry about them. David gives you cause to worry, too. Sometimes he acts crazy—I've seen him try to open the subway doors while the train is still moving. He's also a gymnast, and they can injure themselves.

"My needing some distance doesn't mean that David and I are through. He's going to Bronx Community College this fall, but I've spoken to him about Vanderbilt, and he may transfer there after the first semester. I hope he qualifies for the special scholarship program I'm in. It's called the College Posse, and it's composed of multiethnic and racially diverse students selected by the college.

"Our task is to encourage people of different races and backgrounds to come together. We want to say to the African-American kids, 'We care about you and want to be included in your social and cultural events.' We also want them to say the same things to the white and Asian students.

"You can learn about people from a textbook, but it's better to know them personally. I want to go there as an Asian person and tell them that many people like me exist. The College Posse scholarship program is for kids who have the brains but not the money to go away to college. I think it will be important to my classmates' and my education. It's a first step in our coming together, and I hope David will be there to be a part of it with me."

NINE

Jocelyn Williams

"I was in a special program for gifted students in a mostly white junior high. It was a small school. I felt comfortable there and liked the other students. My best friend was a Greek girl named Lisa.

"I was just beginning to be interested in boys but hadn't dated yet. The only racial tension I felt at that school occurred when I became very friendly with a white boy. Nothing romantic ever happened between us, but some of the white girls resented our closeness. They'd ask me, 'Are you interested in him?' as if I were competition for someone they might want themselves.

"I went on to high school with many of the same people, although our new school was considerably larger. I made the cheerleading squad and found that was a good way to meet people. I had both black and white friends, but by the end of my senior year, I still hadn't dated interracially.

"My friends and I discussed it after seeing an article in *Essence* magazine on 'man sharing'. According to its author, in the future there'll be a shortage of educated, desirable black men due to the large numbers of African Americans who are dying young, involved with drugs, or in trouble with the law. The article indicated that black males who survive the system will be in great demand. Since there won't be enough suitable black marriage partners for all the African-American women wanting them, the writer predicted that many black women will become involved in 'man sharing'. They'll have to share a man with someone else, either knowingly or unknowingly.

"We also talked about this issue at a meeting of our high school's Black Student Alliance. The boys didn't take the threat seriously and joked about how in demand they'll be. The girls were opposed to 'man sharing'. I wouldn't go along with it—that's not the kind of relationship I want for myself.

"I've just graduated from high school, and I'll be going to Syracuse University in the fall. I picked the school for its outstanding journalism department, but I know that only nine percent of its student body is black. There aren't going to be many black guys there to date, so the odds are that I'll be going out with white boys.

"I wouldn't mind dating someone of another race, but I'd prefer to marry an African American. I honestly believe that only a black man can really understand a black woman and the oppression that's a part of our past. Ideally, African Americans should marry one another to preserve our people's heritage and keep our ongoing struggle alive.

"There's also the question of how the important people in your life would feel if you married someone of another race. I know that some of my friends consider it an option, and they'd accept me if I did it. But there'd be others who'd question how I could even go out with a white boy.

"Some black people view interracial dating as rejecting your own people. They think you're not happy with yourself as an African American. I might also feel self-conscious being with a white boy. I'd wonder what his friends might say.

"Still, it's important to me to date boys on my own level, and I know that as I get older, the pool of available black men is dwindling. I don't think I could marry someone whose education wasn't similar to mine or who didn't share my goals and experiences. Someone who made less money than I did might resent me. Many men feel that they have to be the main breadwinner, and a successful woman could be hard for them to handle.

"At the moment, I'm not looking for a relationship leading to marriage. I don't intend to marry until I've finished both college and graduate school. I need this time to accomplish my goals, and I don't want to trade in my dreams for an early marriage.

"When I'm ready to marry, if there isn't a compatible black man in my life, I may end up marrying out of my race. That's because I believe that marriage has to be based on what we feel inside. It's bigger than the black-white conflict—that special relationship has to be built on love and respect. I know that some people can't get past skin color, but I won't close my mind to marrying a white person because of his race. Still, I hope that when the time comes, I find the right black guy." (*Jocelyn went on to college and found the "right black guy."*)

TEN

Victor Castillo

"*I'm sixteen years old and arrived in the United States* from Peru two and a half years ago. People in Peru speak Spanish, but if you're going to live in the United States, you have to learn English. It's important for your survival socially and in school.

"I'll never forget an experience I had on the subway when I first came to this country. I was riding the train with a friend of mine, and at the time neither of us spoke English. A group of young blacks heard us speaking Spanish and began ridiculing us. You didn't need very much English to see that we were the butt of their jokes and gestures. We couldn't have felt more like outsiders.

"I wanted to learn English to fit in. It didn't feel good to be anyone's train ride entertainment. It has nothing to do with having pride in your background and culture. I'm in America now, and English is spoken here.

"I didn't want to go out with girls who only spoke Spanish. The problem was that it's hard to start a relationship with a girl if you only know a few words of her language and she barely speaks yours. That's how it was with my first American girlfriend. She was half Italian and half Puerto Rican, but her Spanish wasn't much better than my English. She lived in our building and was a friend of my sisters. We'd hang out together in the backyard, but there was no chance of our getting serious about each other because we barely communicated.

"Later on I dated a Chinese girl whose family lived in Peru before coming to this country. She was nice, but we weren't together very long. She wanted to be with her friends when I wanted to be with her.

"But a few weeks ago I met a beautiful American dream girl when I represented my high school at a weekend leadership training conference at Marymount College. When I first saw her, I thought, 'God, this girl is so gorgeous.' She had creamy skin, terrific eyes, and long shiny hair. I didn't want to be rude, but I couldn't stop looking at her; I just hoped she wouldn't be mad at me.

"Later that night at the college's dance, I thought I saw her looking back at me. That gave me the courage to approach her and introduce myself. I apologized for staring at her all day, but luckily she was flattered, not angry. She told me her name was Elissa. We danced, talked, and laughed a lot. Elissa and I found that we had so much to say to each other. Learning English these past two and a half years had really paid off.

"As the dance ended, I walked her back to her room. But then I realized that I'd misplaced my own room key. So instead of going to sleep, we decided to hang out together. For the next few hours, we played a game of musical rooms with the conference counselors who monitored the area to see that everyone was in their rooms.

"We ended up in the living room, where we talked until four o'clock in the morning. I felt great being with her and could hardly believe that she was with me. But we were both exhausted, so I walked Elissa back to her room. I still hadn't found my key, but my roommate let me into our room.

"It seemed like I died and went to heaven, but the feeling didn't last very long. The next morning Elissa didn't even look at me. I didn't know what I'd done wrong, but I was sure that it must have been something stupid. I met her at breakfast and said Hi, but there wasn't time to say anything else because we had to participate in a series of conference leadership exercises. After that there was a team debate.

"I was near Elissa all morning, but I didn't breathe easily until she finally sat next to me and took my hand. She put her head on my shoulder, and I knew that things were all right between us after all. I remember feeling glad that she'd been born in America and that I was here now.

"In the afternoon, Elissa and I spent our free time together. Later I met her mother, who'd come to the conference to pick Elissa up. She wouldn't be returning on the bus with everybody else because she had to leave early to go to a wedding. When Elissa introduced me to her mother, I said that she looked more like Elissa's sister than her mother. I wanted to make a good impression on her. I knew how special her daughter was.

"I didn't want Elissa to leave the conference early, and she said she didn't want to go but that she didn't have any choice. I walked her back to her room to get her luggage. We were all wearing the conference T-shirts issued to us, and she said she had to change. I turned my head so as not to watch her as she pulled the shirt up over her head. When she finished dressing, she called me over to her. Then she kissed me.

"I carried her luggage down from her room. I don't know why, but girls always have these big suitcases. Just before we came to the auditorium where her mother was waiting, she kissed me again. We exchanged phone numbers before I delivered her to her mother.

"Elissa left. As far as I was concerned, the weekend was over. She was so pretty and sweet, and now she was gone. I had this terrible feeling in my stomach. My roommate tried to cheer me up. He told me not to worry, reminding me that I could call Elissa the following week.

"You can't imagine how thrilled I was when, after I returned home the next day, Elissa called me! I told her how much I already missed her, and she said that she'd been thinking about me, too. Elissa asked me to pick her up at her school the next day. The day after that was a school holiday, so we went out again. I liked everything about Elissa, and our time together was important to me.

"When I brought her home that night, she said that she'd call me the next day. Everything was wonderful, but at the same time, I was afraid of being too open to her. I didn't want to fall in love with Elissa and get hurt. She already mentioned that she'd be spending the summer with her family on an island. I wondered how it would feel if she went away and forgot all about me.

"The first time I walked Elissa home, I saw that she lived in this big, fancy house on Fifth Avenue. I hadn't known it when I met her at Marymount College, but Elissa was rich. She was this great-looking American girl with everything going for her. I was aware of the fact that I'd been the only Hispanic attending the college conference, and I don't live in the kind of house Elissa does. But we still wound up together, and I hope it lasts."

PART TWO

The Adults Speak

ELEVEN

Barbara Williams

"I've never dated interracially, but in the 1960s when I was in high school, quite a few of my classmates went out with people of other races. I also saw interracial couples in college. Most of them were African-American males with white women. I wondered why these men were dating whites, and I think that they may have had a problem with their self-image. Of course, my view of their behavior stemmed from my own early rearing, and I was raised with a strong sense of African-American pride.

"I married a black man. If a white ever told me that he really loved me, I'd be suspicious of his motives. I know I couldn't help but wonder what was going on in his mind. How could I separate his perception of me from what has occurred throughout our nation's history? Could a white man ever love me for what I am: a black woman? Somewhere in his psyche, would he be looking at me as his slave mistress? It's difficult to live in America and see people for who they really are, because our whole orientation is based on color, class, and gender.

"Many black Americans haven't forgotten segregation, since these experiences aren't that far behind us. My sixty-six-year-old mother has spoken about the limitations placed on her as a black woman during that period. I also experienced blatant segregation as a child during visits to my grandmother and other relatives in the South.

"Once while spending some time at my aunt's Georgia home, I went to the downtown shopping area. I stopped at a luncheonette and was ready to order at the counter when I was told that I couldn't sit there. I didn't believe that this was really happening to me. I lived in New York City and had always taken eating at lunch counters for granted. I also remember going to a southern movie theater and being told that I had to sit in the balcony. Older African Americans in the South dealt with this on a daily basis, and when a black person contemplates dating a white, our collective past has to enter into his or her thinking.

"African Americans who intermarry often meet with substantial opposition. Their choice will usually be more acceptable to the black community. For the most part, the prevalent attitude will be, 'If that's what you want to do, that's fine.'

"But problems are likely to arise when blacks try to cross over into white or Asian settings. I think it basically boils down to skin color. Light skin is supposed to be preferable to a dark complexion. In Cuba, Puerto Rico, and other Caribbean islands, a class system based on color exists as well. If your skin and features are closer to the white European standard, you gain in status. The underlying assumption is that if a person is more white than African, he or she is more intelligent or civilized. This notion, embedded within society's fabric, is difficult to erase.

"It's also important to consider the effects of interracial marriage on children. When a man and woman of different races marry, they don't know if their children will look more black or white. They may have two children, and one may look like the product of an interracial marriage while the other may not.

"My brother once dated a girl whose parents were a racially mixed couple. Her father was a black GI and her mother had been a German war bride. She wasn't sure who she really was and experienced serious identity problems. She was an attractive Hispanic-looking woman with olive skin who could have easily been Italian or perhaps from South America. She dated both white and African-American men but had difficulty fitting comfortably into either circle. She never married.

"My brothers' worlds are more white than mine. That's partly because of their professions. One studied voice and music in college and became an opera singer. There are some African Americans involved in opera, but not many. My brother found few available roles for him and left the profession, realizing that America isn't ready to see a black man make love to a white woman on stage. I doubt whether the country's ready for it in real life either.

"If in the future interracial dating and marriage are more readily accepted, the individuals involved will have to learn to love each other while maintaining a sense of their own cultural identity. If a Japanese and African American want to marry, the Japanese person shouldn't try to culturally become African American, just as the African American should not attempt to be Japanese.

"Instead, each must discover positive ways to share in each other's culture. The simplest means might be food. Both should know and appreciate foods representative of their partner's culture. Basic family values, music, and dance are other vehicles. Crafts are still another area. If you look at baskets from around the world, they're all similar yet distinctively different.

"If we can get past our racial and ethnic differences, we'll finally be free to appreciate one another's human qualities."

TWELVE

Bettye and Haidar Zareaie

Bettye speaks:

"I was one of six children raised in a Christian, Texas family. My interest in boys peaked in my teen years, and I usually dated boy-next-door types. I met my husband [Haidar] while attending college in Arkansas. He was from Iran and was known on campus as a ladies' man. I was more reserved and had a reputation for being hard to get. There were even bets at school as to whether he could get a date with me.

"After getting to know Haidar, I found that we had quite a bit in common. One thing led to another—we began dating and eventually married. Following graduation, we went to live in Iran. I spent a total of four years in my husband's country and another year in Iraq.

"I had to adjust to a very different life-style in Iran. Many American women who followed their husbands there had a difficult time adapting. But I viewed it as a challenge and tried to embrace the people and their customs. I think things might have been easier for me because there was so much about Iran that I genuinely liked. Most of the American women there would meet at one another's homes to complain about how bad things were. I purposely didn't join them because I didn't want to be negatively influenced.

"Instead, I made a real effort to learn the language. My husband brought home a book for me to learn from, and I'd listen carefully to radio and television broadcasts to pick up new words and phrases. I have an ear for languages, and before long I was able to speak to others and make myself understood. This way I could assist my in-laws as well as another family in their daily activities. At one point, I was even held up as a role model for other American wives to emulate.

"While the shah reigned, conditions for Iranian women had begun to improve. Although most older Iranian men thought that wives should be subservient to their husbands, a younger generation who wanted wives as equal partners had begun to emerge. Unlike their fathers, these men didn't find it beneath them to help with the housework. Of course, this was before the 1979 Islamic Revolution, when gender roles became rigidly stratified.

"After we'd been in Iran for two years, my husband went to work for a company with interests in Iraq. His administrative duties required a rotating schedule, with alternating years in that country. Naturally, I moved to Iraq with him, and as I was pregnant at the time, that's where our daughter was born. We lived in the city of Basra, which later became the scene of heavy Allied bombing during 1991's Operation Desert Storm. But it was our misfortune to be there in the fall of 1980, when an eight-year war between Iraq and Iran broke out.

"The borders were immediately closed, preventing us from returning to Iran, and the Iraqi government viewed all Iranians as a security threat. Iraqi soldiers took us, along with seven other families, from our home and placed us under house arrest in another location. Including the children, our group encompassed about twenty-five people; but after about a week, all the men were hauled off to prison. Some were tortured, since Iraqi intelligence officers thought they might have valuable information.

"My daughter and I were released from house arrest after about a month and a half, and when my husband returned from prison, we decided to immediately leave the country. Our escape route took us through Kuwait to Pakistan before reaching Iran.

"We stayed in Iran for another year before deciding that the baby and I should go back to the United States. Iran had changed considerably. Now the government forbade women to work outside the home. Even if my husband died, I wouldn't be able to get a job to support my child and myself. I'd be forced to rely on my brother-in-law to provide for us. My daughter also wouldn't be able to enroll at a university when she came of age. We didn't want our child to grow up this way, and these factors entered into our decision to leave Iran.

"I was lucky to be able to exit the country. Back then Iran was not permitting Americans to leave, but as I'd married an Iranian, I had dual citizenship. Nevertheless, I wasn't allowed to take any money out of the country. My family had to send the funds for our journey home, and my baby and I left Iran with only the clothes on our backs. When I arrived in the United States, we lived in Memphis, Tennessee, with my mother until we could be reunited with Haidar in America.

"Leaving Iran was much more difficult for my husband. After returning to Iran from Iraq, he was imprisoned in his own country because he was suspected of being an Iraqi sympathizer. Once my husband was released, he still wasn't allowed to leave the country. Ironically, Haidar was eventually permitted to go because he'd married a foreigner.

"If I could relive my life, I don't know if I'd make all the same choices. There are definite advantages to marrying someone from another culture. Learning a new language and traveling to a distant part of the world are enriching experiences. But if you want to travel and know other cultures, you don't necessarily have to get married to do so.

"However, I wanted to marry someone as committed to family life as my husband is. Strong family ties are characteristic of his culture. My Iranian in-laws were wonderful. Haidar's family treated me like a daughter. My family wasn't very tightly knit during my formative years, and I knew that when I had my own family, I'd want the special closeness that my husband brought to ours.

"I think that religious differences between couples can usually be worked through. I'm Christian and my husband is Muslim. We're raising our children as Christians, but we're also exposing them to the Muslim faith. We don't place one religion above the other. We've explained to our children that all religions are merely different ways of worshiping the same God.

"That's not to say that there aren't special strains in

an intercultural marriage. Many of our Iranian friends who married American women experienced difficulties. While these men chose to relocate to the United States, they often retained an extremely strong attachment to their country and experienced an inner conflict over leaving it. Some couples have even tried to go back and forth between countries.

"I know how difficult it must be for the person who leaves his or her homeland. I love Haidar's family and missed them terribly when I left Iran. I only spent a few years there, but I still remember all the positive aspects of Iranian culture. Of course, when I was in Iran, I missed my own family; and when I was pregnant, I'd have killed for a taco.

"American women who marry Iranian men probably have a higher divorce rate than women married to Americans. Any American who wants to marry a man from another culture should think carefully about what she's doing. Some men propose to American women just to get a green card, so they can permanently live and work in this country. Even if the man sincerely loves her, she should question whether his feelings for her are stronger than his bond to his country and all that he has left behind. In such situations, it's important to be guided by your mind as well as your heart."

Having traveled extensively, Bettye's husband Haidar concluded that dating people who are different from ourselves can have far-reaching ramifications. As he remarked, "Everyone's views are broadened by learning about new cultures either through marriage or friendships. It's unrealistic to think that we are ever going to join together to become 'one world'. We speak too many different languages and have too many diverse ways of doing things. In some nations, people eat dogs, while that notion is abhorrent in other places.

"The real challenge is not to use our differences as a means to reinforce existing prejudices. If we could view others with greater tolerance, governments might be influenced by our sentiments and eventually achieve greater peace and stability in the world."

THIRTEEN

Betty Lee Sung

"I wrote a book on Chinese-American intermarriage, and my research indicates that it's on the rise. Intermarriage is a fairly recent phenomenon in the Chinese-American community. This may be partly because until 1967 it was illegal in fourteen states for Asians to marry Caucasians. Another reason may be that the Chinese community in the United States was very small until relatively recently. Before 1965, only 105 Chinese people were allowed into the country each year.

"Intermarriage may have also increased due to civil

Author's Note: Betty Lee Sung chairs the Department of Asian Studies at the City College of New York. She is the author of numerous books and articles on the Chinese-American experience.

rights legislation, which opened doors that had been formerly closed to the Chinese. They entered schools and occupations they'd been barred from and increasingly came in contact with people of different races. Many intermarriages took place among individuals who met in college. Academic campuses frequently generate a more open and accepting atmosphere than is generally found in society. College students also relate to one another on equal footing.

"Most of the interracial couples that I interviewed started out looking for someone of their own background. Many believed that they'd eventually marry someone similar to themselves but instead met other people who satisfied their emotional needs. It may have had something to do with the low number of available young Chinese people in this country.

"Although older Chinese Americans have expressed their concern over what they perceive as a rapidly growing trend toward intermarriage, in actuality, the rate is not as great as many believe. In my research, I looked at over 150,000 marriage license applications. I was surprised to find that in New York City, the intermarriage rate is only twenty-seven percent, compared to forty-one percent in Los Angeles and seventy-six percent in Hawaii. For some other Asian groups, such as the Koreans and Japanese, the rates of intermarriage are much higher. This may be because Chinese people are more traditional and tend to cling to their own beliefs.

"A number of intermarried Chinese Americans found religious differences between themselves and their spouses to be not as troublesome. Chinese people are generally very tolerant of other religions. They don't care how you worship: The more religions you practice, the better a person you are. But other religions tend to be more monotheistic: You have to believe in God as they perceive him and worship in a prescribed manner.

"My research indicated that resistance to intermarriage was usually strongest among Chinese and Jewish families. A young Jewish man and his Chinese wife endured a rageful response from the man's mother. She was so opposed to the marriage that she threatened not to come to the wedding. Her daughter finally persuaded her to attend, and she showed up at the last minute.

"In other instances, a potent resistance to intermarriage has emanated from Chinese-American families. A Chinese woman bitterly protested her daughter's marriage to a white man. She refused to call her son-in-law by his name, and whenever her friends asked her who he was, she'd simply answer, 'A friend.'

"Nevertheless, the woman lived with her daughter and son-in-law and cared for their children. Her son-in-law treated her very well, and her daughter felt that after a time the mother came to love him. However, she still never acknowledged him to the outside world. A number of my Chinese acquaintances have also refused to publicly recognize their intermarried sons or daughters-in-law.

"I was born in the United States, and being second-generation Chinese, I'm far more open to intermarriage than my parents were. If I ever told them that I wanted to date interracially, they'd have never allowed it. They were very strict and had even wanted to arrange a marriage for me. But I resisted their efforts and later married a Chinese man of my own choosing. Today I have eight children, and three of them have non-Chinese spouses. I would have preferred them to marry Chinese Americans, but that's not what happened.

"I don't feel that intermarriage results in a loss of

status any longer, but I know that intermarried couples have to face some unavoidable hassles. Whether or not you like it, it's bound to happen when someone in the family looks different from everyone else. This is especially true in Chinatown [New York], where interracial couples may be stared at and jeered. Even if the remarks aren't always overtly hostile, you can easily find yourself in an uncomfortable situation.

"Things become further complicated once there are children. Children of mixed marriages may not be sure of where they belong. Some are ashamed of their Chinese background and would rather identify with the whites. They may find themselves wishing that their parents never married.

"In discussing Chinese-American intermarriage, we tend to think of white and Chinese unions. Yet my research clearly shows that Chinese people in the United States have also married blacks, Puerto Ricans, Mexicans, Japanese, and others. I didn't come across any group that was particularly accepting of intermarriage. I guess most groups feel more comfortable around people who are like themselves. In cases where both families were adamantly opposed to the marriage, often the couples called off the wedding. I believe it takes a strong person to cope with the additional burdens intermarriages frequently entail.

"But despite the problems involved, I think that intermarriage will continue. It's almost inevitable as long as people freely mingle. In an open society, diverse people will always find one another."

FOURTEEN

Linda and Garth Marchant

Linda speaks:

"As a young person, I lived in an African-American neighborhood but attended a predominantly white school. It was among the top public schools in the city. My mother purposely enrolled me there to get the best education possible. When I was in second or third grade, she sent me to the store and realized that I couldn't calculate how much change I had coming. At that point, she knew that I had to go to a better school.

"In junior high school, most of my girlfriends were African American, although I had some white friends, too. However, by the mid-1970s, when I went to high school, the races began to separate. The blacks largely hung out by themselves, and the whites went their own way. We'd had some race riots, and you stayed with your own kind since there was safety in numbers. No one was sure when violence might break out.

"I managed to maintain friendships with some whites I'd known for years, realizing that not all the whites or blacks had been involved in the racially motivated incidents. But even though not everyone sympathized with the rioters and rock throwers, their actions could touch any of our lives at any time. Once while some African-American students boarded the buses to leave school, a group of angry whites began throwing rocks at us. One girl was so badly hurt that she went to the hospital.

"Tempers were short, and at any moment, emotions could flair. Black and white kids might be playing ball together, and if one called the other a name, they'd start fighting. Before long their rage might spread to other members of the community. It was just one of those things.

"I wasn't seriously dating at the time, but I'd go to movies or parties with African-American boys. In the eleventh grade, I began seeing an African-American college student. He took me to campus parties, and going out with him made me something of a celebrity at school. Dating a college man afforded me status, but that didn't make it a satisfying relationship. I was just sixteen while he was twenty-one, and he continually tried to control my life.

"I didn't notice a significant amount of interracial dating during this period. Some African Americans and Hispanics went out together, but blacks who dated whites usually did so secretly. African Americans openly involved with whites often contended with caustic remarks from other blacks. They'd say things like, 'You think you're so high and mightly and too good to associate with us.' It was difficult for blacks dating whites to avoid that kind of thinking in their own neighborhoods.

"After graduating from high school, I attended York College. Ninety percent of the students there were black, about eight percent were white, and the rest were Asian. At college, interracial couples dated freely. In an academic environment, they didn't encounter the same degree of friction I'd witnessed in high school.

"Yet in college I realized that you don't have to date someone of another race to experience cultural differences in interpersonal relationships. I had begun dating a man from Haiti. Both Haitians and African Americans are of African descent, but there are differences between us. Haitian culture is very strong, and Haitians have some definite ideas about what a woman should be. Instead of looking for a typical American woman, they usually prefer to be with a more passive female companion. They don't even like women to drive cars. They perceive it as giving us an opportunity to drive away from them.

"The Haitian student I went out with was extremely old-fashioned and believed that a woman's place is in the kitchen. I used to ask myself, 'Why is he dating me?' We were both involved in student government, and I was president of the association. We worked together, but I think he would have preferred to be president instead of having a woman in charge.

"He wasn't right for me. After we broke up, I dated several men from different African countries. The African men I went out with were extremely generous. They'd give you the world if they could. One of them was a Nigerian who imported and exported medical supplies. All the lovely material things he gave me were nice, but our cultural differences made me leery of becoming deeply involved with him.

"Some African men grow up in polygamous African

societies and already have several wives before coming to America. I'd heard stories about these men marrying American girls without telling them about their wives back home. They also believe in having substantially large families. I couldn't see myself marrying a man who wanted at least ten children.

"I didn't marry the Nigerian, but I didn't choose a native-born American either. My husband originally came from Jamaica, and I met him at a political convention in upstate New York after he'd been here a number of years. Following the convention, he had begun calling me regularly, and at first I actually believed he just wanted to discuss politics.

"But I was happy to learn otherwise. He was tall, handsome, and as interested in political issues as I was. Of course, I knew there had been some friction between the Caribbean blacks like my husband and American-born blacks. A sizable number of blacks from the Caribbean had come to the United States in the 1970s and opened businesses. They took full advantage of the available educational opportunities to advance themselves. At times, African Americans were forced off jobs by Caribbean workers willing to accept lower wages. Many Caribbean blacks did extremely well fairly soon, and some African Americans resented their quick success.

"While dating my husband, I asked him why he chose an American woman rather than a Jamaican one. He told me that he didn't care about a woman's country but was just interested in being with a good person. Still, after getting to know my husband and meeting some of his Jamaican friends, I couldn't help but notice differences between Caribbean black men and African Americans.

"Jamaican men are generally more jealous and possessive. They also rely more heavily on the extended family—a tradition that stems from African culture. They expect grandparents to be much more involved in raising their children than most African Americans. My husband and I have discussed sending our children over to their grandmother's house on a regular basis. But I don't want my parents to take on this additional responsibility at their age. We have three children, and I feel it's our duty to raise them on our own.

"There's also a difference in the degree to which Jamaican men help their wives with the housework and child care. Before we had children, my husband never cooked or cleaned. But with three youngsters, he and I both realized that there was just too much for one person to do. Now we share the chores, and my husband acknowledges that it takes two to make things work.

"I have two daughters, and I'm teaching them to be assertive instead of modeling themselves after a more passive Jamaican feminine ideal. Women who aren't independent and prepared for a career feel helpless if the man they're with leaves. I want my daughters to be strong, self-reliant women regardless of whom they marry.

"My experiences show that cultural differences between a man and a woman can be overcome through communication and understanding. As long as the couple is basically compatible and both individuals care about each other and the marriage, they can make a go of it."

Linda's husband, Garth Marchant, also had some interesting experiences involving interracial and multiethnic relationships. He attended a college near the Canadian border in Oswego, New York, where only 10 percent of the school's student body was African American and Hispanic, while the rest was white. As he recalled, "As far as I know, only one black family lived in the area, and all minority group students experienced some degree of racism. When we wanted black history courses incorporated into the curriculum, the college administration denied our request. The local law enforcement officials were especially racist in their treatment of us. Whenever black students shopped in the town's stores, the sheriff would arrest them as though they were about to commit a robbery.

"I was active in the campus student association and had been seeing a white girl who was also involved in student activities. We liked each other, but as soon as she brought me home to meet her parents, I knew it was over between us. They didn't approve of her dating a black, and apparently she was not about to defy them.

"Coping with discrimination at Oswego strengthened me as a person. I grew committed to lessening the existing tension between the minority group students and the community. I worked with the local cable television network to establish a cultural exchange program to expose residents to black and Caribbean cultures. It was important to emphasize that every group has something of value to offer.

"Before long our efforts resulted in some visible changes. We developed a better understanding with the sheriff's staff as they became convinced that we weren't a threat to them. Our minority students' union operated a hot line with the sheriff's office to work out any disputes that arose. We'd effectively demonstrated that we weren't there at their expense and that we deserved to be respected and heard.

"After college I dated African-American women as

well as some women from other cultures. My wife, Linda, is an African American, but she could have had any background. We just related well to each other and wanted to spend the rest of our lives together.

"It's important for black people to appreciate their history and culture, but I don't believe that racial or cultural biases should influence an individual's choice of his or her mate. When it comes to a romantic relationship, love is the bottom line. I don't see that as a betrayal of black culture. You have to keep too much hate inside yourself to automatically rule out worthwhile exchanges between different races and cultures."

FIFTEEN

Rev. David Aaronson

"I came to Sparta, New Jersey, from Newburgh, New York—a multiracial community on the Hudson River. During the twelve years I was a pastor at Newburgh, I never officiated at an interracial wedding, which surprised me since our church was in a black neighborhood.

"When I arrived in Sparta twenty-three years ago, it was lily-white and very Waspy. I therefore found it ironic that I had a request for an interracial marriage my first month here. It came from a white girl in our congregation who wanted to marry a young black engineer she'd met in college. I saw nothing wrong with the marriage and proceeded to make the usual counseling appointments we schedule prior to a wedding.

"During the planning stage, however, we heard from

the couple's parents. The boy's mother and father were comfortable with the marriage and fully accepted their son's bride. The girl's mother felt torn over the interracial aspect of her daughter's relationship, while the bride's father was outspoken in his opposition to the marriage.

"The couple went ahead with their plans despite her father's objections. They were married in what I felt was a nice ceremony. The groom's family was there in good number and was clearly happy for the couple. Part of the bride's family attended, but it was obvious that some family members, including the bride's father, were absent.

"There had also been some opposition to the marriage from several members of the church. I hadn't expected to find that residue of resentment in such an affluent and sophisticated congregation. But those individuals hadn't been involved in interpersonal black and white relationships and obviously just didn't know how to respond. In some ways, the wedding proved to be a learning experience for them.

"I've kept track of that young couple through the years. He's still with his company and she teaches nursing. They live in upstate New York and have two lovely children. Their eldest daughter just began college this year. I see them when they come back to Sparta to visit.

"The bride's mother eventually decided to back her daughter in her decision, but the girl's father continued to disapprove of his daughter's marriage and acted hostilely. When his daughter wanted to visit, he'd tell her not to bring her husband along.

"After the birth of the couple's first child, the woman's father mellowed somewhat, although he never fully accepted his son-in-law. Things had improved when he suddenly died in his late fifties from a massive heart attack. Fortunately, his reconciliation with his daughter began before it was too late.

"There generally appears to be more opposition to black-white marriages than to other types of interracial unions. The black-white marriage I described took place over twenty years ago, but I don't think we've made very much progress in improving interracial relations since then. In recent years, we've witnessed racial problems in Crown Heights and Bensonhurst, New York, as well as in other parts of the country.

"However, there are some steps an interracial couple planning to marry can take to ease the way. Young people dating individuals of another race often go to great lengths to keep this from their parents. Their families may have no idea of their intentions and may react poorly to a sudden engagement announcement.

"If a couple involved in an interracial or interreligious relationship feel their families will oppose them, they should begin to build the bridges of reconciliation early on. Talk to your parents about your feelings as soon as possible. Naturally, they'll try to talk you out of it and offer a hundred reasons why you shouldn't marry Mr. or Ms. X. But there's a far better chance of remaining close if the lines of communication are open.

"It's easier for a parent with reservations about mixed marriages if the child approached the parent and said, '____ and I are serious about each other and are thinking about marriage. How do you feel about that?' As a pastor, I'd then have an opportunity to work with the parents ahead of time and help them to be supportive of their offspring's decision. But if a mother or father is presented with the child's plans as an accomplished fact, he or she can easily become defensive.

"It's also important for engaged interracial and interreligious couples not to live in a dream world. Through counseling sessions, they can learn how to best deal with discrimination they may encounter. I usually project some test cases. For instance, before black-white marriages were as accepted as they are today, I might ask mixed couples how they'd handle being seated in a back booth near the kitchen in a restaurant. Would they immediately realize that they have consumer rights? Would they protest the inappropriate treatment?

"They need to think about how they'll deal with situations involving children. How would they feel if their son or daughter came home from school crying after being teased about being the product of a mixed marriage? Would they be enraged and hurry off to the principal's office to create a scene? Or would they assess the situation with the teacher to see if a positive class lesson could be devised to ease tensions?

"It's important for interracial couples to realize that the road ahead may be rocky and that they need to be prepared. They have to learn to meet negative experiences in a positive way. In some instances, religious differences have been as problematic as racially mixed unions. I just performed a Christian-Jewish wedding a few months ago. The couple was very open about their feelings, and their families approved of their choice of partners.

"But even under the best circumstances, it's wise for interreligious couples to explore some central issues prior to marriage. Hanukkah and the Christmas season usually arrive at about the same time of year. How do they intend to celebrate? Will the couple choose one religion for them both, or will they go their separate ways? These are practical considerations that need to be addressed, and ideally these issues should be worked out before there are children.

"One good strategy for interreligious couples who can't agree on a common place of worship is to participate at each other's places of worship. It's important for each to support his or her partner. Holiday seasons frequently have a nostalgic quality, and people tend to reminisce about the past holidays with their families. Each spouse should learn about the other's holy days and be sensitive to his or her beliefs.

"Some interreligious couples hope to expose their children to both religions and allow them to choose for themselves. This may sound like a fine idea, but it rarely works. Usually in these instances, neither parent takes the responsibility for fully introducing the child to his or her faith. A young person cannot make a sound choice if he doesn't know as much as he needs to about what he's choosing. If couples want their family to practice one religion but can't find any common ground between them, they might consider joining a Unitarian church—its approach is prayer to one God.

"Things can also be done on a community level to ease the way for both interracial and interreligious couples. The more exposure community groups have to different cultures and the greater the dialogue between them, the better the chances for good relations.

"Today many more people are enlightened about interracial and interreligious love and marriage than in the past. But we still have a long way to go."

Further Reading

BOOKS

Almonte, Paul, and Theresa Desmond. *Interracial Marriage.* New York: Crestwood House, 1992.

Anastos, Phillip, and Chris French. *Illegal.* New York: Rizzoli, 1991.

Anderson, Elijah. *Streetwise: Race, Class, and Change in the Urban Community.* Chicago: University of Chicago Press, 1990.

Bender, David, ed. *Immigration.* San Diego: Greenhaven Press, 1990.

Chan, Sucheng. *Asian Americans: An Interpretive History.* Boston: Twayne, 1990.

Davis, F. James. *Who Is Black? One Nation's Definition.* University Park: Pennsylvania State University Press, 1991.

Davis, Marilyn P. *Mexican Voices, American Dreams: An Oral History of Mexican Immigration to the United States.* New York: Holt, 1990.

Gay, Kathlyn. *The Rainbow Effect: Interracial Families.* New York: Franklin Watts, 1987.

Good, Kenneth, and David Chanoff. *Into Their Heart: One Man's Pursuit of Love and Knowledge Among the Yanomama.* New York: Simon & Schuster, 1991.

Lemann, Nicholas. *The Promised Land: The Great Black Migration and How It Changed America.* New York: Knopf, 1991.

Mathabane, Mark, and Gail Mathabane. *Love in Black and White: The Triumph of Love Over Prejudice and Taboo.* New York: HarperCollins, 1992.

Mura, David. *Turning Japanese: Memoirs of a Sansei.* Boston: Atlantic Monthly Press, 1991.

Parks, Gordon. *Voices in the Mirror: An Autobiography.* New York: Doubleday, 1990.

Powledge, Fred. *Free at Last? The Civil Rights Movement and the People Who Made It.* Boston: Little Brown, 1991.

Rosenberg, Maxine B. *Living in Two Worlds.* New York: Lothrop, Lee & Shepard, 1986.

Sung, Betty Lee. *Chinese American Intermarriage.* New York: Center for Migration Studies, 1990.

Vital, David. *The Future of the Jews.* Cambridge: Harvard University Press, 1990.

Yep, Laurence. *The Lost Garden.* New York: Julian Messner, 1991.

ARTICLES

Brokaw, Renee. "You Can't Join Their Clubs: Six Mixed Couples Get Together to Talk About Love, Marriage, and Prejudice." *Newsweek,* 10 June 1990, 48.

Goldman, Ari L. "Polls Show Jews Both Assimilate and Keep Tradition." *New York Times,* 7 June 1991, 14A.

Jeffries, Dexter. "Who Am I?" *Present Tense,* July-August 1988, 49.

Randolph, Laura B. "Black Women/White Men, What's Goin' On?" *Ebony*, March 1989, 154.

Turner, Renee D. "Interracial Couples in the South: Attitudes Are Changing on Once-Illegal Marriages of Blacks to Whites." *Ebony*, June 1990, 41.

Weathers, Diane. "White Boys." *Essence*, April 1990, 64.

Index

A

Aaronson, Rev. David, 89–93
African Americans, 1–9
   antiwhite feelings of, 24
   and dating whites, 20, 82–83
   friction with Caribbean
      blacks, 84
   and Hispanics, 82
   and Japanese Americans,
      13, 15
   and Malaysians, 51–55
   middle class, 5, 9
   northward migration of, 4
   shortage of men among, 58
   views on interracial dating,
      59
   women, 21–22
Age, 45
Aggressiveness, 32
Amnesia, see Social amnesia
Asian Power movement, 15–16
Asians, 9–16
   stereotypes associated with,
      43
   see also Chinese; Japanese
      Americans; Vietnamese

B

Basra (Iraq), 72–73
Bethel College, 5
Bigotry, see Racism

Black Power movement, 7–8
Black separatism, 8
Brazil, 47
Bronx (New York City), 43
Bryne, Hazel, 6
Buffalo (New York), 3

C

California, 10
Carmichael, Stokely, 8
Castillo, Victor, 61–64
Celebrities, 5
Chang, Ai-De, 27–30
Child care, 85
Children, 5, 20, 69, 80, 92
   see also Custody
Chinatown (New York City), 80
Chinese, 77
   discrimination against, 10
   and Hispanics, 37–39, 48–49
   and Jews, 79
Christianity, 74
Christmas, 92
Civil Rights Act (1964), 7
Civil rights movement, 7
Class system, 68–69
   see also Status
College, 83
College Posse (Vanderbilt
      University), 55
Colombia, 31–32, 48
Color, 22

About the Author

Elaine Landau received her B.A. in English and Journalism from New York University and her master's degree in Library and Information Science from Pratt Institute.

Ms. Landau has worked as a newspaper reporter, an editor, and a librarian, but feels that many of her most fascinating moments have been spent writing over fifty books for young people. Other books by Elaine Landau for Julian Messner include: *Child Abuse, An American Epidemic, Revised Edition; Different Drummer, Homosexuality in America; The Homeless; On the Streets, The Lives of Adolescent Prostitutes; Teenage Violence; Teenagers Talk about School;* and *Why Are They Starving Themselves?, Understanding Anorexia Nervosa and Bulimia.*